Dangerous SPIDERS

AN IMAGINATION LIBRARY SERIES

Funnel-Web
SPIDERS

by Eric Ethan

Gareth Stevens Publishing
A WORLD ALMANAC EDUCATION GROUP COMPANY

Please visit our web site at: www.garethstevens.com
For a free color catalog describing Gareth Stevens Publishing's
list of high-quality books and multimedia programs,
call 1-800-542-2595 (USA) or 1-800-387-3178 (Canada).
Gareth Stevens Publishing's fax: (414) 332-3567.

Library of Congress Cataloging-in-Publication Data

Ethan, Eric.
  Funnel-web spiders / by Eric Ethan.
    p. cm. — (Dangerous spiders—an imagination library series)
  Summary: An introduction to the physical characteristics, behavior, and life cycle of
funnel-web spiders.
  Includes bibliographical references and index.
  ISBN 0-8368-3767-3 (lib. bdg.)
  1. Agelenidae—Juvenile literature. [1. Funnel-web spiders. 2. Spiders.] I. Title.
QL458.42.A3E83   2003
595.4'4—dc21   2003045555

First published in 2004 by
Gareth Stevens Publishing
A World Almanac Education Group Company
330 West Olive Street, Suite 100
Milwaukee, WI 53212 USA

Text: Eric Ethan
Cover design and page layout: Scott M. Krall
Text editor: Susan Ashley
Series editor: Dorothy L. Gibbs
Picture research: Todtri Book Publishers

Photo credits: Cover © ® Jean-Paul Ferrero/AUSCAPE; p. 5 © Jack Green;
p. 13 © Kathie Atkinson /AUSCAPE

Printed in the United States of America

1 2 3 4 5 6 7 8 9 07 06 05 04 03

**Front cover: Everything about a Sydney
funnel-web spider is big and dark — and
its bite can be deadly!**

TABLE OF CONTENTS

Words that appear in the glossary are printed in **boldface** type the first time they occur in the text.

SYDNEY FUNNEL-WEB SPIDERS

One creature that nobody in Australia wants to run into is the Sydney funnel-web spider. It is one of the most dangerous spiders in the world. Its bite can cause serious illness — even death. Although Sydney funnel-webs and humans try their best to stay away from each other, the spiders sometimes wander into people's houses. Fortunately, the people who live in and around Sydney, Australia, have learned to watch out for funnel-webs.

Watch out! Reared up with its two front legs in the air and showing its powerful fangs, this Sydney funnel-web spider is ready to strike.

WHAT THEY LOOK LIKE

Sydney funnel-webs are big spiders. The body of an adult female can be 2 inches (5 centimeters) long. Males are a little smaller. Both males and females have smooth bodies and hairy legs.

At the end of a funnel-web's **abdomen** are two fingerlike **spinnerets**, which the spider uses to spin silk. All spiders have spinnerets, but, on most spiders, they are too small to see. The spinnerets on a Sydney funnel-web are large and easy to see.

Sydney funnel-webs also have large **fangs**. Their fangs are so powerful they can easily bite through a person's fingernail!

Sydney funnel-web spiders range in color from dark brown to glossy black, but they all have dark purple abdomens.

HOW THEY GROW

As for any other kind of spider, life for a Sydney funnel-web begins in an egg sac. After **mating**, a female Sydney funnel-web lays about a hundred tiny eggs and wraps them in balls of silk, called egg sacs, to protect them. She hides the egg sacs in her **burrow** and guards them until the eggs hatch, which takes about three weeks.

Even after the eggs hatch, the **spiderlings** stay in the egg sac for a while. They **molt**, or shed their outer shells, at least once before leaving the egg sac.

For the first few months of life, Sydney funnel-web spiderlings stay with their mothers. Then they leave to make homes in burrows of their own.

Intruders, beware! A female Sydney funnel-web spider will defend her egg sac against anyone or anything that threatens to harm it.

Sydney funnel-web spiderlings are fully grown in two to four years. Adult females might live another ten years, but they will spend most of that time inside their burrows. Female funnel-webs rarely leave home. Adult males, on the other hand, become permanent wanderers. They might live another six to nine months, and most of that time is spent looking for females and mating.

Male funnel-webs do most of their wandering at night, especially during the warm months of spring and summer. It is at these times that funnel-web spiders are most likely to wander into people's yards and houses.

These funnel-web spiders are mating. A male funnel-web (on the left) has a short adult life, so it must mate as often as possible.

WHERE THEY LIVE

Sydney funnel-web spiders live only in Australia, within 100 miles (160 kilometers), in any direction, of the city of Sydney. Almost four million people live in this area on Australia's southeastern coast, so it is very likely that humans and spiders will meet.

Funnel-webs sometimes build their burrows near people's houses, often in their gardens. These spiders especially like moist or damp areas. They have even been known to fall into people's swimming pools!

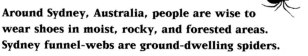

Around Sydney, Australia, people are wise to wear shoes in moist, rocky, and forested areas. Sydney funnel-webs are ground-dwelling spiders.

THEIR WEBS

Funnel-web spiders build their homes in sheltered places, such as in deep cracks between rocks or holes they dig in the ground. They spin funnel-shaped webs that lead into dark, hidden burrows. Instead of staying on the web, the spider lives in the deepest part of the burrow, where it is moist and cool.

At the entrance to the burrow, the spider spins long strands of silk, called trip lines, that spread out in all directions. A trip line acts like a doorbell. When an animal steps on one, the spider knows it has company.

The silk trip lines stretching outward from this funnel web form an alarm system for the spider living deep inside the burrow.

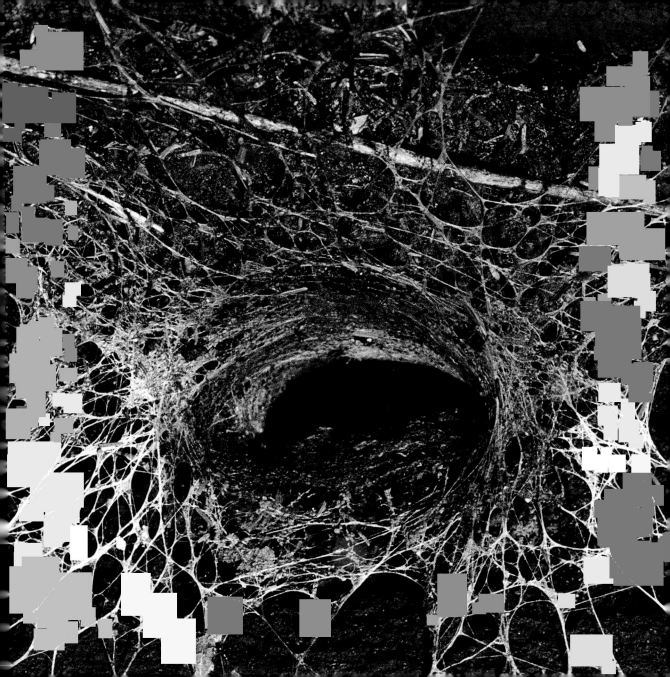

HUNTING FOR FOOD

The typical diet of a Sydney funnel-web spider includes beetles, cockroaches, and other insects. But these spiders have also been known to eat larger animals, including frogs and lizards.

When it comes to getting a meal, a funnel-web spider is very **patient**. It hides at the back of its burrow, waiting for **prey** to pass by. The minute something hits a trip line, the spider races out of the burrow. If that "something" is good to eat, the spider grabs it and bites it. The funnel-web's powerful fangs **inject** a deadly poison, or **venom**, that kills the prey. Then, the spider drags its meal into the burrow to eat it.

Peeking out of the opening to its burrow, a
Sydney funnel-web spider patiently watches
and waits for prey to touch a trip line.

THEIR BITES

Sydney funnel-webs are **aggressive** spiders so they are more likely to bite than to run away, especially if they feel threatened. Both males and females are poisonous, but males are the most dangerous. A male funnel web's venom is five times stronger than a female's and contains a chemical that is highly poisonous to humans. Also, because of the males' wandering habits, they are more likely to come into contact with people.

The bite of a male funnel-web spider can make a person very sick in just minutes. An **antivenin** can block the effects of the poison, but the person must receive the antivenin right away, or the bite could be **fatal**.

Positioned to strike, this female Sydney funnel-web spider looks ferocious, but a wandering male is actually more dangerous.

THEIR ENEMIES

Lizards and birds prey on Sydney funnel-web spiders. These kinds of animals are able to strike quickly, before the spider can fight back. Humans, however, are a funnel-web's greatest enemy.

Seeing deadly spiders anywhere near their homes is bound to frighten people, so Australians living in and around the city of Sydney do everything they can to get rid of them. To avoid **predators** and other dangers, male funnel-webs usually stay hidden during the day and wait until dark to wander in search of females.

The worm coming out of this Sydney funnel-web is a parasite, which means that it has been feeding on the spider's body tissues.

MORE TO READ AND VIEW

Books (Nonfiction) *I Didn't Know That Spiders Have Fangs.* Claire Llewellyn
(Millbrook Press)
Life Cycle of a Spider. Ron Fridell and Patricia Walsh
(Heinemann Library)
Mighty Spiders! Fay Robinson (Scott Foresman)
Spider. Killer Creatures (series). David Jefferis and Tony Allan
(Raintree/Steck-Vaughn)
The Spider. Life Cycles (series). Sabrina Crewe (Raintree)
Spider's Nest. Watch It Grow (series). Kate Scarborough (Time-Life)
Spiders Spin Webs. Yvonne Winer (Charlesbridge)
Spotlight on Spiders. Nature Close-Ups (series). Densey Clyne
(Gareth Stevens)

Books (Fiction) *Charlotte's Web.* E. B. White (HarperCollins)
Once I Knew a Spider. Jennifer Owings Dewey (Walker & Co.)
The Spider and the Fly. Mary Botham Howitt (Simon & Schuster)
Spider Weaver: A Legend of Kente. Margaret Musgrove and Julia
Caims (Scholastic)

Videos (Nonfiction) *Bug City: Spiders & Scorpions.* (Schlessinger Media)
Nightmares of Nature: Spider Attack. (National Geographic)
See How They Grow: Insects & Spiders. (Sony Wonder)

WEB SITES

Web sites change frequently, so one or more of the following recommended sites may no longer be available. To find more information about funnel-web spiders, you can also use a good search engine, such as **Yahooligans!** [www.yahooligans.com] or Google [www.google.com]. Here are some keywords to help you: *dangerous spiders, funnel-webs, poisonous spiders, spider bites, spiders.*

homepage.powerup.com.au/~glen/spider.htm

This colorful and intriguing web site is largely the result of work done over several years by fifth grade students at Rochedale State School in Australia. A scroll down the page reveals icon after icon to click for photos, facts, first-aid, and fun. When you visit this site, be sure to click on the icon for "Australian Spiders - Funnel-web" for information about, as well as some fantastic color photos of, Australia's most poisonous spider.

www.amonline.net.au/spiders/dangerous/funnelweb/

For clear, straightforward, easy-to-navigate information about funnel-web spiders, this web site is one of the best. After a brief description of the funnel-web family, you can click on links to pages about their homes, their habits, and how to handle their bites. Make sure you don't leave this site until after you've visited the "Suspects Gallery." It has some great close-ups of both funnel-webs and funnel-web look-alikes.

www.backyardnature.net/spidsilk.htm

Funnel webs are the first to be described on this page about "Spider Silk." Although the spider that spun the web pictured is not a "Sydney" funnel-web, you will get a good look at what a funnel-web's web looks like. Then, you can compare it with descriptions and photographs for sheet webs and cobwebs. This page also describes other uses for spider silk and gives a brief description of spider anatomy.

www.termite.com/spider-identification.html

Keep an eye on the male funnel-web in this site's lineup of the dangerous dozen. He's one of twelve venomous spiders, presented four across, in three rows, for easy identification. Click on either of the funnel-webs to find out just how "deadly and aggressive" they are. You can click on "First Aid," too, — just in case! At the end of the information for all twelve spiders, one more click will take you to the "Spider Identification Chart." It ranks the venomous spiders from deadly to low-risk. Guess which spider tops the chart!

GLOSSARY

You will find these words on the page or pages listed after each definition.
Reading a word in a sentence can help you understand it even better.

abdomen (AB-doh-men) — the back half of a spider's body, which contains its spinnerets, eggs, heart, lungs, and other organs 6

aggressive (uh-GRES-iv) — bold and forceful, usually the first to attack or start a fight 18

antivenin (an-tee-VEN-in) — a kind of medicine that helps prevent venom from causing painful wounds, illness, or death 18

burrow (BUR-roh) — a hole in the ground, usually dug by an animal 8, 10, 12, 14, 16

fangs (FANGZ) — long, pointed teeth 4, 6, 16

fatal (FAY-tl) — causing death 18

inject (in-JEKT) — to force a liquid into body tissues through a sharp, pointed, needlelike instrument 16

mating (MAYT-ing) — joining with a male to produce young 8, 10

molt (MOHLT) — shed a covering, such as skin, on the outside of the body 8

patient (PAY-shunt) — able to wait for a long time without becoming annoyed 16

predators (PRED-a-ters) — animals that hunt and kill other animals 20

prey (PRAY) — (n) an animal that is killed by another animal for food 16; (v) to hunt and kill for food 20

spiderlings (SPY-dur-lingz) — baby spiders 8, 10

spinnerets (spin-nuh-RETS) — fingerlike organs at the back of a spider's abdomen, which the spider uses to make silk 6

venom (VEN-um) — poison that an animal produces in its body and passes into a victim by biting or stinging 16, 18

INDEX